Post-War Britain Resource Book

Contents

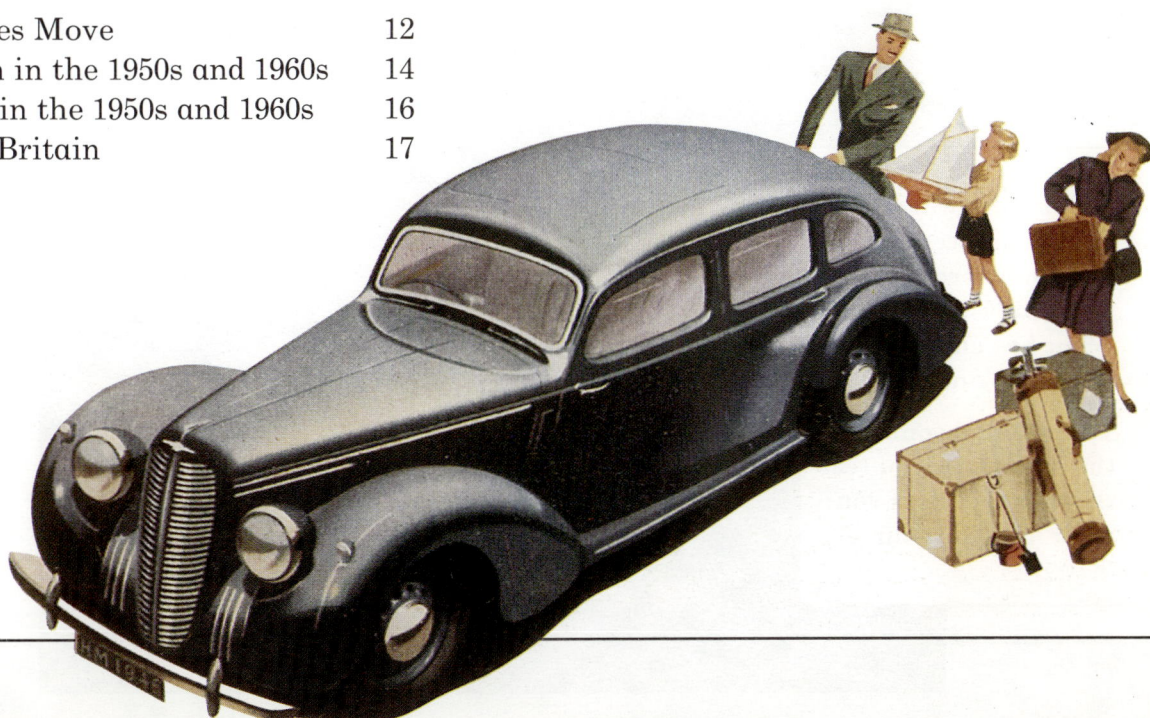

Britain after the War

What Happened after the War?

The time between the end of the Second World War and now is often called post-war Britain. Some people find it hard to think of their own time as 'history', but when they look back, they can see that many things have changed since they were young. Perhaps you can find someone who will tell you about the time after the war.

You may belong to a family that moved from one part of the world to another. You may live in a house that was not even built when the war ended in 1945.

Perhaps the biggest change of all has come with the introduction of television into our homes.

How is post-war Britain different from Britain before the war in the 1930s?
What has changed since 1945 and why?

You will find some of the answers if you read this book. Others you must look for yourself.

A New Government

The first thing to change when the war was over was the Government. In May 1945 a General Election was announced. People still in the **forces** had to have a postal vote. The result could only be announced in July, when all the **ballot boxes** arrived back in London from overseas.

On this page are two election posters from 1945.

♦ What do you think the big V sign made people think about?

♦ Did any part of the poster remind them of the war? Which part?

♦ Which part of the poster made them think about the future?

♦ How has the artist used colour to make this look better than the war part of the picture?

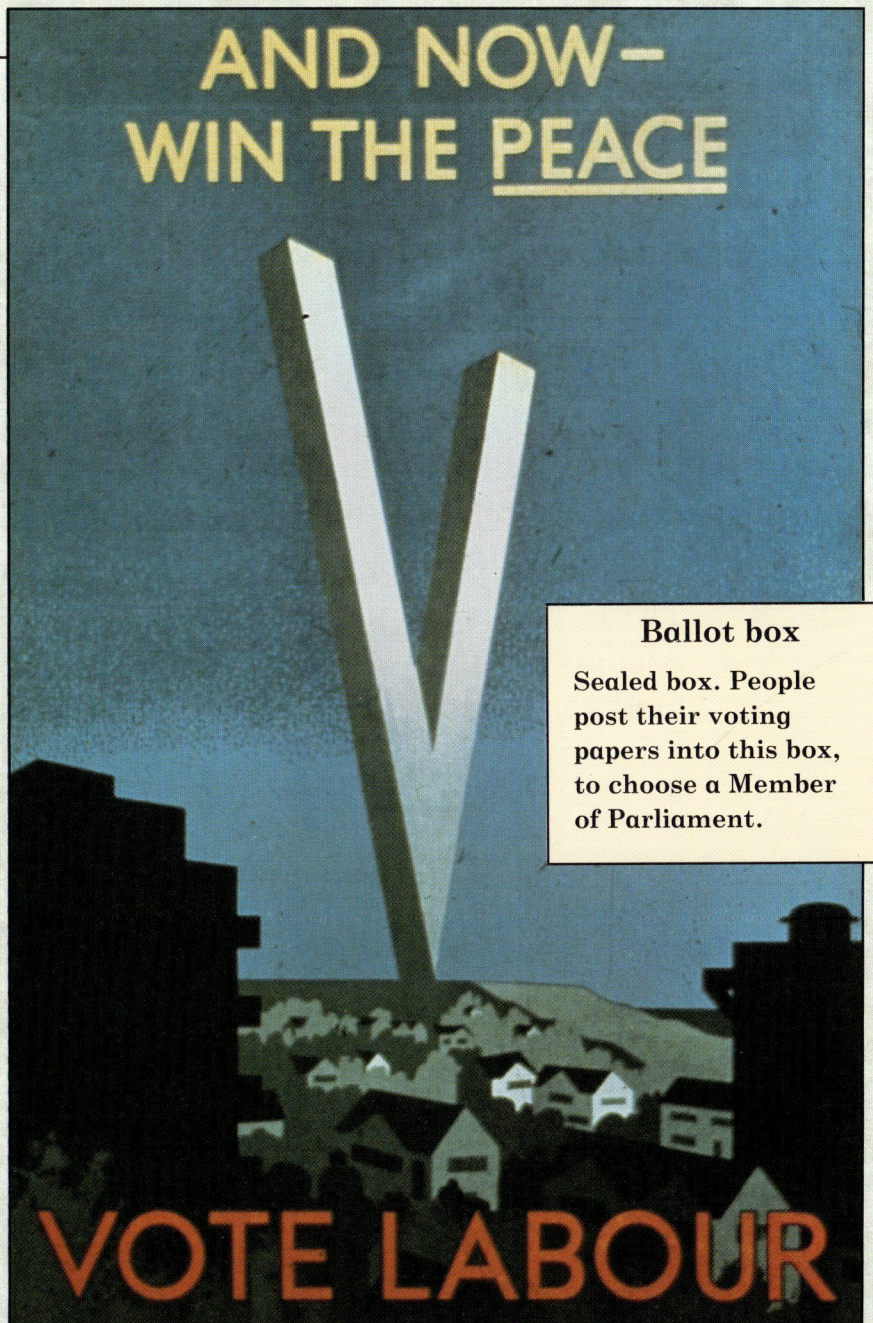

AND NOW — WIN THE PEACE

VOTE LABOUR

Ballot box

Sealed box. People post their voting papers into this box, to choose a Member of Parliament.

LET'S BUILD THE HOUSES—QUICK !

Vote LABOUR X

Why was the promise to build houses quickly one which attracted voters immediately after the war?

The Labour Party won the election, with more votes than any party had ever had. This meant that Winston Churchill, the great war leader, was no longer Prime Minister.

Forces

People in the army, navy and air force.

3

Post-war Homes

Prefabs and Tower Blocks

Thousands of new homes were needed when the war ended to replace those that had been bombed in the war. The men and women who had fought in the war came home to Britain. They wanted to settle down, find somewhere to live and have a family. The need for new homes was urgent.

These houses show you one way the Government solved the problem. They are called 'prefab' homes which is short for prefabricated. It means that all the parts of the house were built in a factory. They were delivered by lorry and put up very quickly, a bit like making a model when all the pieces have been cut out for you.

Can you see where the pieces join in this picture?

Prefabs were not very sturdy. They were only meant to last for ten years, so there are not many about nowadays, only pictures of them.

When the Councils had more time, they built homes which have lasted until today.

Tower blocks like these were built in many big cities. They were built from steel and concrete.

Can you see the prefabs in front?

They were built of wood and a material called asbestos. After a few years they got old and damp and the families moved into the flats. Some people liked the flats; some preferred the old prefabs, even if they were not very well built.

Suppose you were in a family who moved from the prefabs to the flats:

♦ How different do you think life was?

♦ What sort of view was there from their windows in the prefabs and the windows in the flats?

♦ What sounds do you think they heard in each place?

♦ What did they have in the prefabs but not in the flats?

♦ What did they have in the flats but not in the prefabs?

New Estates

In the 1950s there was a **baby boom**. Lots of people wanted family-sized houses. Housing estates like this one were built all over Britain. Lots of people still live in houses built in the 1950s.

The houses were built of brick and had tiled roofs. The windows had metal frames. There was plenty of space between them and they all had a garden.

One woman who moved into a new house like this in the 1950s remembers that it was,

"... absolutely beautiful even though there were no garden paths but planks up to the front door.".

Some of the streets on the estates were named after Second World War leaders. Can you find out who they were?

CHURCHILL ROAD

MONTGOMERY ROAD

TEDDER WAY

BEVIN DRIVE

Baby boom

A time when lots more babies were born than in most years. Why do you think this happened once the war was over?

Bypass
Road taking traffic around, not through the town.

'New' Towns

Some of us live in post-war 'New' Towns. The first one was called Stevenage and builders started work on the town in 1948. When they arrived there was nothing but farmland although the 'New' Town had been carefully planned on paper. The first families moved in before everything was built.

Look at these children going to school with their mum in 1954.

♦ Look carefully at the background in the photograph. How can you guess that this is a 'New' Town?

♦ How far away do you think the school is?

Planning a 'New' Town from the beginning meant that there could be different areas for homes, schools, shops, factories and offices.

On the plan, find:

♦ where the homes and schools were built. There were six different neighbourhoods.

♦ where the factories were built.

♦ where the main roads were planned.

♦ where the bypass road was built.

What has not been put on this plan that would be put in a town plan today?

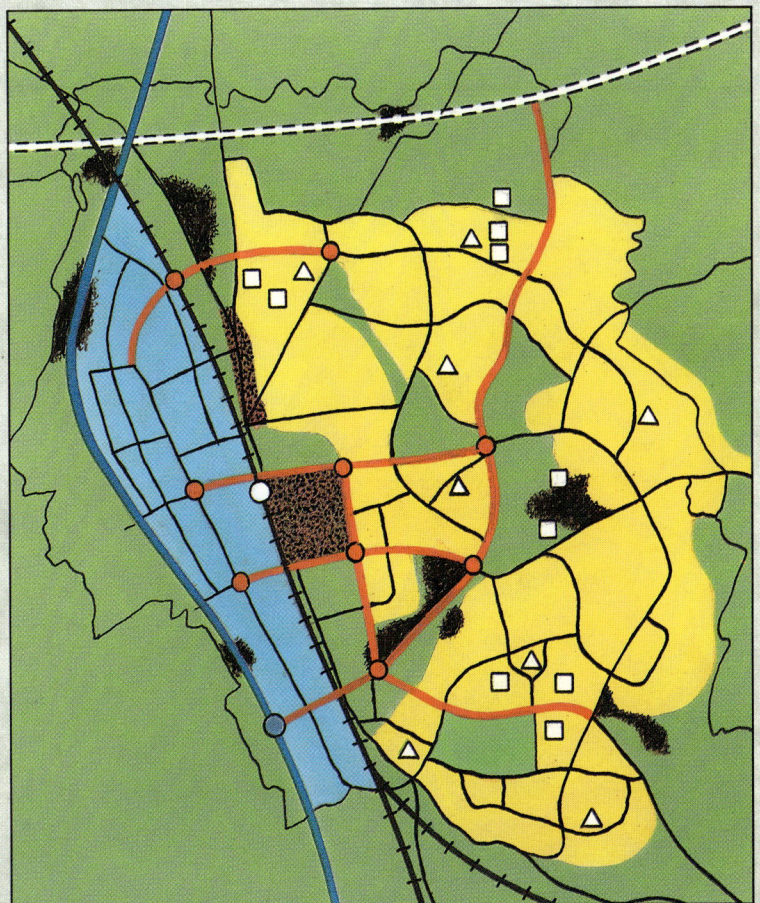

▢ Residential areas (yellow)	○ Railway station
Town centre	⊢⊢⊢ Railway
Employment area (factories)	Farmland or open space
△ Primary school	Woodland
▢ Secondary school	Bypass
	— Main roads

Here is a photograph of Stevenage taken in 1958.

Find:

◆ the road for cars.

◆ the cycleway.

◆ the footpath.

◆ the grassed area.

Do you think this area was well-planned or that space was wasted?

Lots more 'New' Towns were built after Stevenage. This map shows you where the 'New' Towns were built.

◆ What parts of the country were they built in?

◆ Why do you think this was?

Milton Keynes is the most recent 'New' Town. Many of the planners' good ideas which were first built in the 'New' Towns have now been built in many of our old towns:

— Shopping centres for **pedestrians** only.
— Cul-de-sacs to stop cars driving through areas where people live.
— Bus lanes.
— Industrial and business parks, where people go to work.
— Trees and grass to make the place look nice.
— Community Centres and Health Centres.

This is a shopping centre in Milton Keynes.

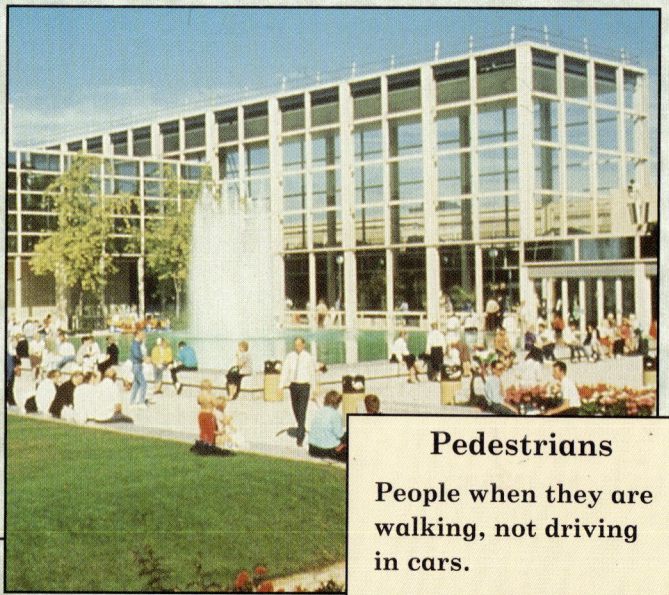

Pedestrians

People when they are walking, not driving in cars.

Hard Times and the Festival of Britain

Hard Times

Perhaps you think that once the war was over life improved for everyone. This is not quite right. For most people the years 1945 to 1951 were hard ones. They are sometimes called the years of **austerity**.

Britain had spent a lot of money on the war. Food and clothes were still rationed. A bad winter in 1947 stopped the trains and buses. Fuel and food could not be moved round the country.

> **Austerity**
>
> A difficult time when things people needed were in very short supply.

These people queued up to buy coke in London. They took it home in their prams and homemade barrows. They needed it to heat their homes.

♦ How do you think their lives compared with the lives of the people in the 'New' Towns?

The Festival of Britain

The first 'New' Towns were one sign that Britain was beginning to recover from the shortages of the war years. Another was a big celebration in 1951 called the Festival of Britain. It was designed to help people think about the future instead of looking back to their difficulties in the war and immediately after.

One government minister said that people should give themselves 'a pat on the back'. What do you think this meant?

This was one of the special Festival of Britain stamps.

♦ Can you see the Festival sign on both the book and the stamp?

♦ Have you seen it anywhere before?

In this picture you can see the skylon, a silvery object made of aluminium which seemed to float in the air.

There were Festival events all over Britain. There were big exhibitions and events in cities like Belfast, Cardiff, Edinburgh and in smaller towns and villages. Look around where you live. If you see the Festival sign you will know that it is a clue about your town or village in 1951.

The Festival of Britain exhibitions gave people a chance to see examples of modern engineering and design.

This was the new style in furniture.

Find:

♦ the light coloured wood.

♦ the shape of the chairs and table.

♦ the pattern on the carpet and curtains.

♦ the room divider.

♦ the low light over the dining table.

What is missing from this living room?
Does it look very modern today?

> **Room divider**
>
> A set of cupboards or shelves which divided one part of the room from the other.

Families on the Move

Why do Families Move?

Thousands of families have moved from one home to another since the end of the Second World War. Perhaps your family is one of them.

Living in Britain today are many people who chose to live and work here. Living in Australia, France and Spain are other people who chose to leave their homes in Britain. They all moved for one of the reasons on the list below.

You want an adventure.
You want to live where the weather is better.
You want to live near other members of the family.
Unpleasant, even cruel things, are happening to your family where you live now.
Someone is offering cheap fares if you go to their country.
You hear that there are better jobs with more pay somewhere else.

♦ Why do people move?

♦ Which of the reasons written here would make you want to move?

Here are some of the reasons people gave when asked about moving in an **oral history** interview;

Mr Sodhi who moved from India to Coventry.

> "The idea of moving to England came really from dad. He always wished that one member of the family should go abroad. I was a teacher in India, and the British Government were sending vouchers for teachers to come over, so I applied and got a teaching voucher."

Mrs Shiokkas, whose father moved from Cyprus.

> "He came in 1947. He left Cyprus because everyone was so poor and they thought they would come to England to help the family. They all had British passports and Britain wanted them to come and work. So this was the natural place to go."

> **Oral history**
> History collected from a series of interviews.

This family moved to Britain like Mr Sodhi, Mrs Shiokkas and Mrs Ma.

Mrs Ma moved from Guyana. Like many other people she had a British passport as Guyana is one of the countries in the British Commonwealth.

> "I came to Britain because I wanted to see a new country, get some experience, restart life all over again. Other countries didn't attract me. No, I could contribute here because it was a British country and I was British. I still am."

Liner
A very big ship which carries passengers.

Immigration in the 1950s and 1960s

In 1956, three thousand new settlers a month arrived in London from the Caribbean. They travelled across the Atlantic Ocean on a **liner** and took the train from Southampton to London.

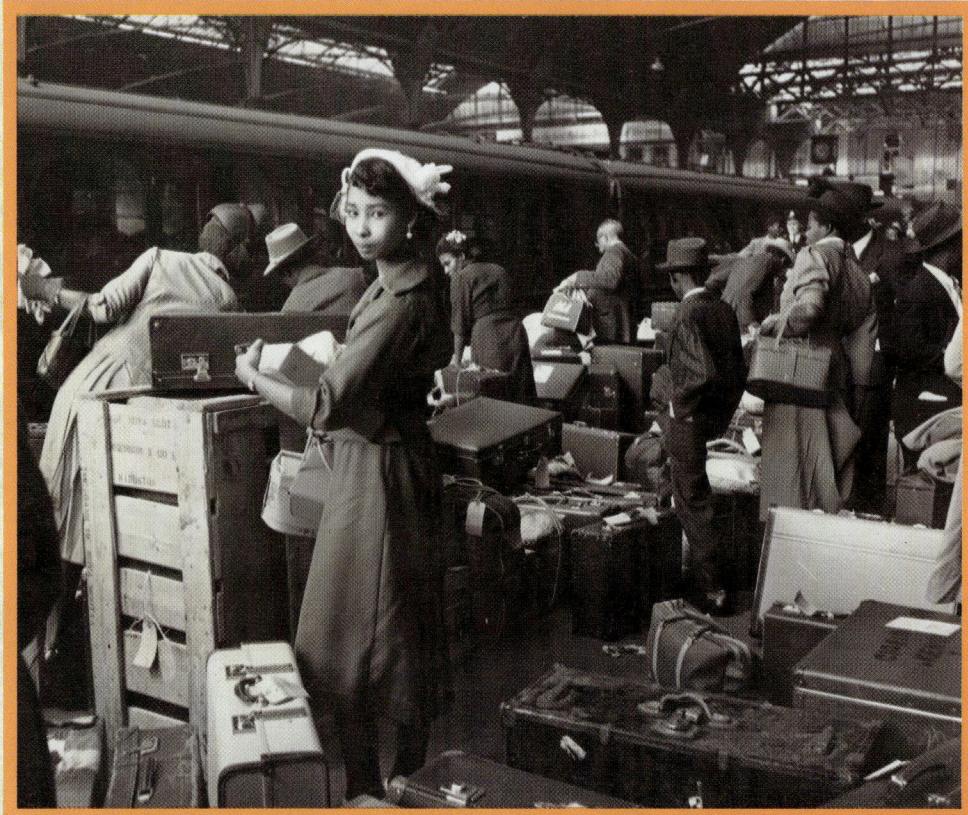

NORTH AM

N

→ Immigration

◆ **Do you think they are wearing their best clothes or work clothes?**

◆ **Is there anything about their clothes to tell you if it was hot or cold when they left Jamaica?**

◆ **Have they got much luggage? Remember they have decided to live and work in Britain.**

◆ **What do you think is in the woman's big box?**

◆ **How do you think she is feeling?**

Immigrants like these filled important jobs in Britain; in the hospitals, on the railway and buses. London Transport managers travelled to the Caribbean to recruit this woman. This means she knew she had a safe job in Britain, even before she left home.

Immigrant
A person who leaves one country to settle in another.

This woman collected fares on London buses.

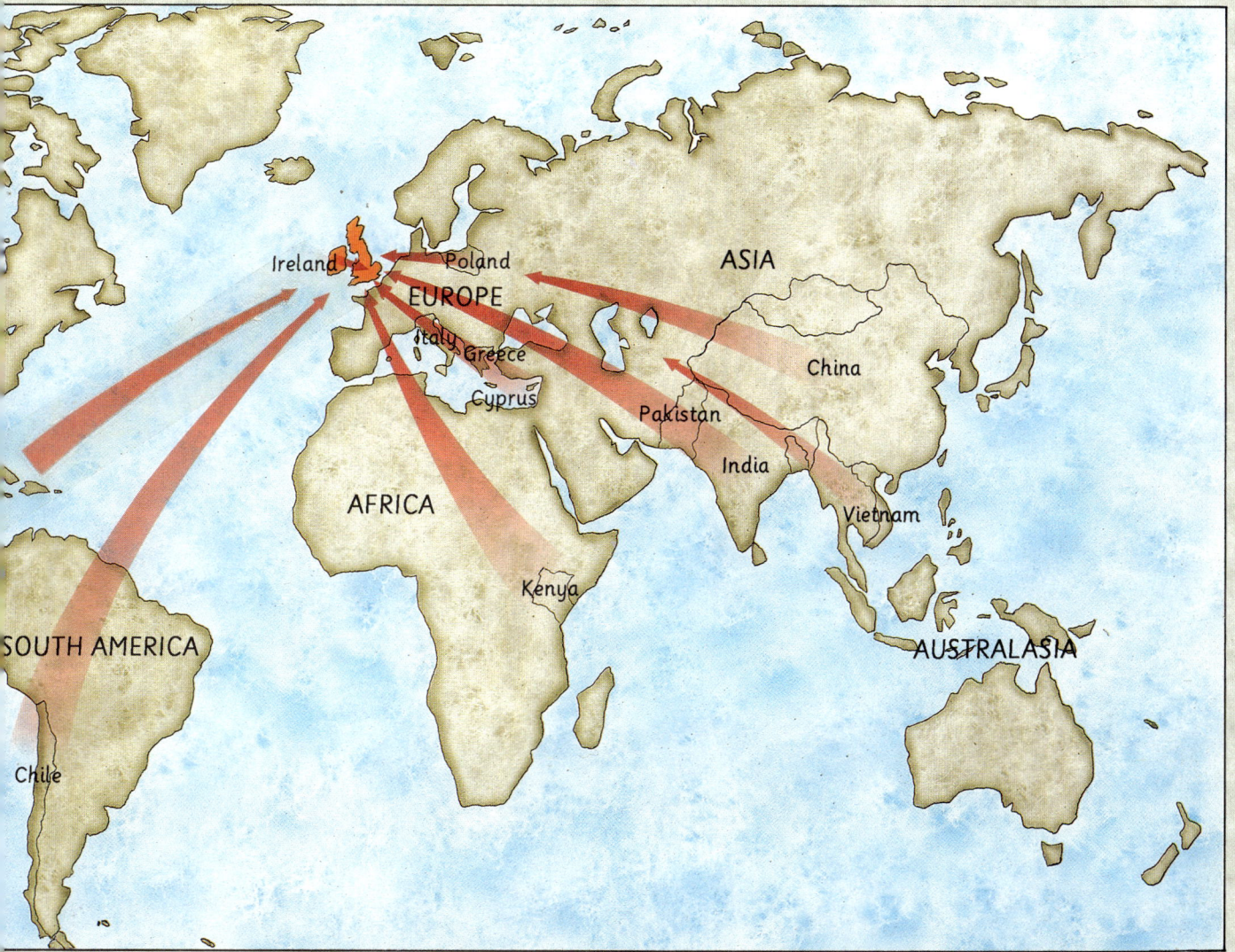

Immigrants came from all over the world. You can see where they came from on this map.

Most of them did not stay in London for long. They joined families and friends already settled in Birmingham, Manchester, Leeds, Leicester, Glasgow and other big cities. Their families helped them find a job and a home.

Some opened shops or restaurants selling the food they had eaten at home. They helped change the British taste in food. Now we all eat Italian, Chinese, Greek and Indian food and it can be bought in almost every town and supermarket.

Where did most immigrants come from?

Which of the foods below have you eaten?

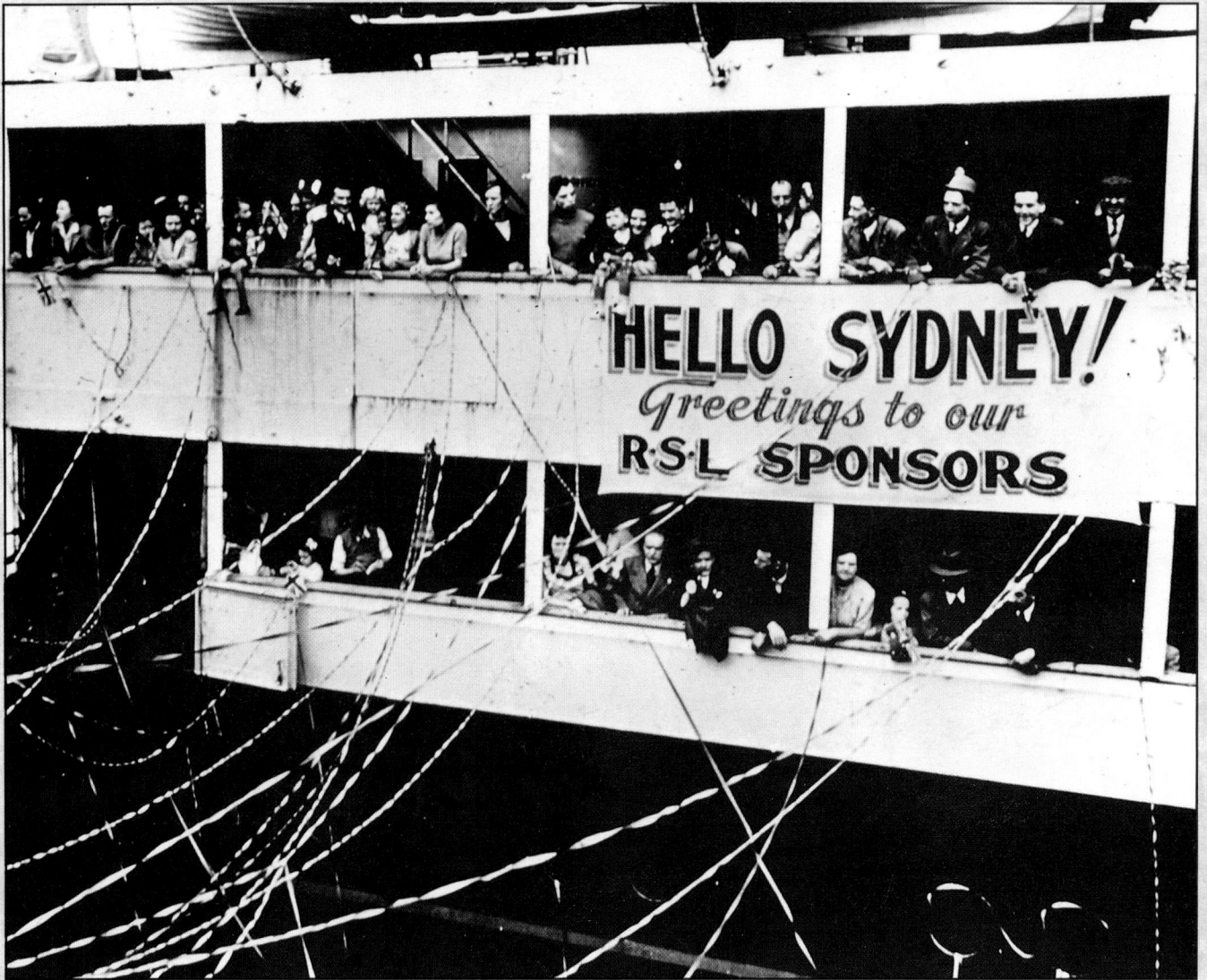

Emigration in the 1950s and 1960s

The money for these people's fares came from the Retired Serviceman's League.

Many white Europeans emigrated in the 1950s and 1960s, particularly to Australia. They liked the sound of Australia because:

— The weather was warm and sunny for most of the year.

— Australia is a big continent. There was enough spare land for migrants interested in farming to buy land of their own.

— The Australian government only asked them to pay £10 for their fare.

Like the Jamaicans, the first families to go travelled by sea on big liners. When they arrived they were housed in hostels and helped to find a home and a job.

In the 1980s and 1990s some Britons moved to France and Spain. At first they used their new homes for their holidays but many now want to live in Europe all the time. They hope to travel to France easily by using the Channel Tunnel.

Changes in Britain

Newcomers to a country usually make life there more interesting because of the customs and **traditions** they take with them

Festivals, like Divali, Chinese New Year and Carnival are now celebrated in Britain. Irish groups, like this one, meet to play Irish music, particularly on Saint Patrick's Day.

One of these men is playing a fiddle which is like a violin. Fiddles are traditional Irish instruments.

People who move to new homes also want to have their own church, mosque or temple. The first Muslims and Sikhs to settle in Britain had to build their own. This was very important because:

— They wanted to pray in the same way as they had always done.

— They wanted to celebrate traditional festivals like Divali.

— They wanted somewhere to have weddings and funerals.

— They wanted their children and grandchildren, who were born in Britain, to learn how to be a Muslim or Sikh, like their parents and grandparents.

Most towns now have a mosque or temple. This was not the case in the 1940s and 1950s.

This mosque was built in Regent's Park in London.

Traditions

Beliefs and customs handed down from one generation to another.

British Industry and Transport

Cotton

Since the Second World War there have been many changes in people's working lives. In some years there has been a **boom**; in other years there is a **slump**.

Some new mills were closed soon after they first opened as it was cheaper to buy cloth from places outside Britain than to make it here in Lancashire. A boom somewhere else in the world meant there was a slump in Britain.

Boom
When there are plenty of jobs.

Slump
When there are few jobs.

This is just one of the old cotton mills that was closed down around 1950. The machinery was over a hundred years old.

Here is a new mill with its modern machinery. How many workers can you see?

Coal

The coal mines were the first thing to be nationalised. This meant that the Government bought them from private owners so that any profits could be used for the benefit of everyone in the country.

Once the Government owned the coal, which was needed to make electricity and gas, they planned to provide cheap power. They thought this would help everyone working in British industry.

This man is looking at the new board put up outside a coal mine or colliery on the day it was nationalised.

◆ **Can you read the notice?**

◆ **What do you think the man is thinking?**

◆ **Do you think it made a difference if the colliery was managed by the owner or by workers in the National Coal Board?**

THIS COLLIERY IS NOW MANAGED BY THE

NATIONAL
COAL BOARD

ON BEHALF OF THE PEOPLE

JANUARY 1ˢᵗ 1947

At first the nationalisation of the coal mines was very successful.

Some of the improvements the National Coal Board made were:

— New machinery to cut the coal.

— Electric **conveyor belts** so that the coal was sent up from under the ground more quickly than before.

— Miners were paid a proper wage for a day's work, instead of being paid for the amount of coal they brought to the surface.

— There were new safety rules for workers underground.

— There were new bathrooms so that every miner could have a bath before going home at the end of his shift.

> **Conveyor belt**
> Like the checkout in a supermarket. The coal was moved along by electricity.

This is what one miner remembered about the change:

"And when I went home nice and clean, the wife didn't know where she was because before that I used to have a bath in front of the fire in an old tin bath.".

The improvements meant they were able to persuade more people to become miners. They produced more coal than was actually needed.

These miners have just come up from the mine.

What do the safety notices say?

But coal is a very dirty fuel. When it burned, the smoke made the buildings black. When oil and natural gas were discovered under the North Sea in the 1960s, people wanted to use them instead of coal partly because they were clean fuels and did not make so much smoke.

So pits began to close. In 1957 there were 833 collieries but in 1970 there were only 293.

Now lots of mines have been closed. In some parts of Wales, Durham and Scotland, it took time before new factories were built and many people were out of work.

This was the first power station to make electricity from nuclear fuels, it was opened in 1956.

♦ Can you see how clean it looks?

The new factories made cars, aircraft and electrical goods. The newest factories of all make computers.

These men make microchips for computers in South Wales, where there were coal mines in 1945.

Suppose you were writing the history of the last hundred years in this area. What would you say had changed?

Railways and Roads.

One of the biggest changes in post-war Britain has been the way people travel and transport heavy goods.

In 1945 you could travel anywhere in the country on the railway. Trains were pulled by steam engines and even small towns had their own station. Special goods trains carried heavy things like coal, building materials, farm animals and some food.

In the towns everyone used trams or trolleybuses and there was still horse-drawn traffic in some places.

This is why things changed. Six different factories made cars in Britain in the 1950s. Together they built forty different models. Many were exported all over the world while Japan and Germany were still recovering from the war. Now it is the Germans and Japanese who make most of the cars.

This type of train was common in the years just after the war. Now they are very rare. Have you ever travelled in one?

The Hillman Minx was made in Coventry. Which customers are they trying to attract in this advertisement?

For the motorist whose car is always in use

HILLMAN MINX

A PRODUCT OF THE ROOTES GROUP

Look at this picture of the first motorway in Britain, the week before it was opened in 1959. It cost 22 million pounds to build and was the first road to have three lanes. It was 72 miles long and went from London to Birmingham. Three thousand cars used it in the first two hours.

Why do you think the man had to sweep the road?

As more people and goods began to use the roads, the railways began losing money.

Between 1958 and 1963 nearly 4,000 railway stations and 5,000 miles of railway track were closed.

Here are some other things that happened as a result of these changes:

— Big container lorries carried goods that had once gone by rail.

— More motorways were built through the countryside.

— The car industry expanded and more people bought cars.

— Parking became a problem. Big car parks were built in the centre of towns and parking meters were put up in the streets.

Look at this picture. The railway line has gone and the station is closed.

Air Travel

Another industry that has grown since the war is the aircraft industry. Even when the war was over, new fighter planes were being built. This was because there was a 'Cold' War.

There were two sides in the 'Cold' War. Britain, Western Europe and America were one side. Russia and Eastern Europe were on the other. Each side made weapons to threaten the other side but they never actually used them. That is why it was called the 'Cold' War.

The government was also keen for more **civil aircraft** to be built.

Concorde was designed to fly faster than the speed of sound. It was built by the British and French as a joint project and had its first test flight in March 1969.

Later in 1969, an American, Neil Armstrong, was the first **astronaut** to land on the moon.

One result of the growth of the aircraft industry was that more planes were built for the holiday trade. Holidays abroad became much cheaper in the 1960s. People bought 'package' tours for the first time. The holiday price included the air fare and somewhere to stay.

This is a picture of Concorde. It meant that people could travel around the world faster than ever before.

Civil aircraft
Planes built for passengers not for war.

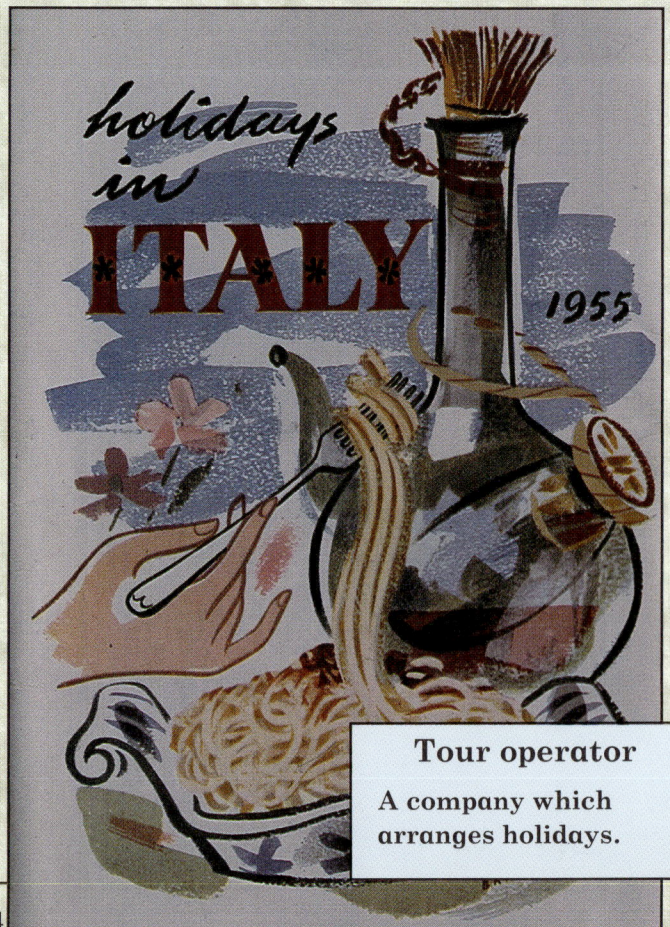

holidays in ITALY 1955

How are the tour operators trying to persuade customers to go to Italy in this advertisement?

Tour operator
A company which arranges holidays.

Astronaut
Space pilot.

More air transport meant that more airports had to be built. Heathrow Airport in London was opened in 1946.

This picture shows Heathrow being opened.

Now there are airports all over the United Kingdom. This map shows where some of them are. Is there one near you?

Aberdeen

Glasgow

Belfast

Newcastle

Liverpool

Manchester

Birmingham

Luton

Cardiff

Stansted

Heathrow (London)

Gatwick

Life at Home

Life at home changed more quickly during the 1960s than in any other decade in post-war times. Wages rose faster than prices and there were lots of **consumer** goods in the shops.

When he wanted to be re-elected, the Prime Minister, Harold Macmillan told people,

"You've Never Had it So Good.".

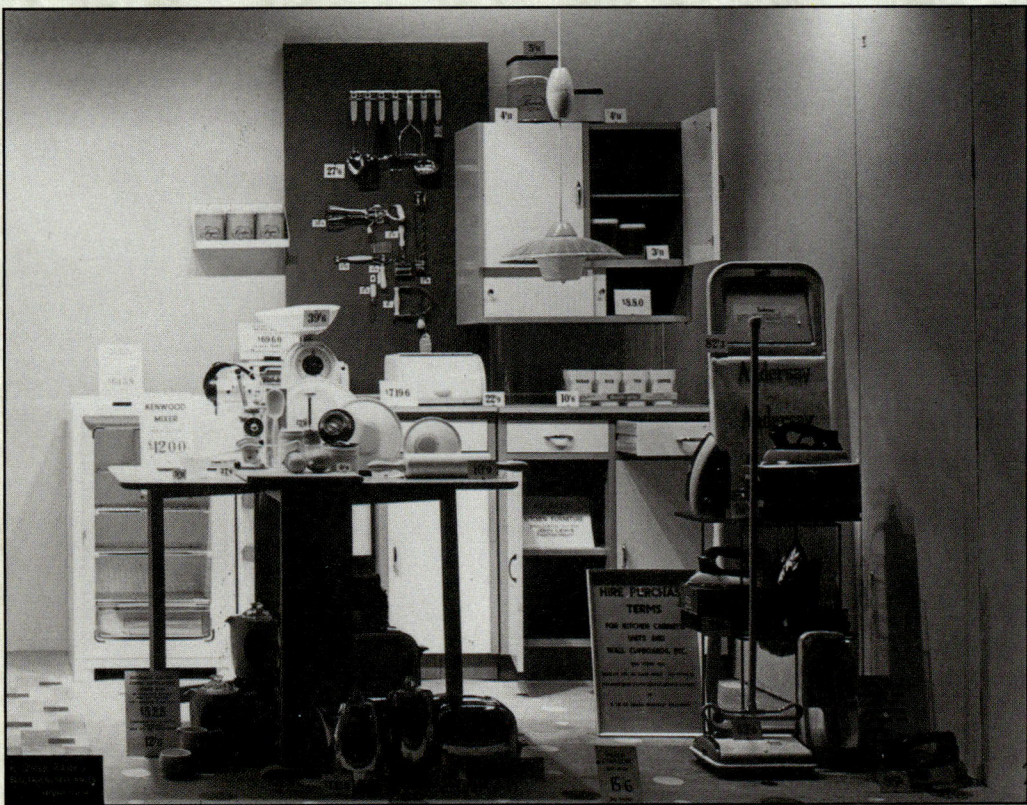

Here are some of the things people were able to buy then. Find:

♦ electrical goods for the kitchen.

♦ a refrigerator.

♦ a modern ceiling lamp.

♦ an electric iron and ironing board.

How do you think these things changed the lives of people in the 1960s?

Consumer

Another name for a customer, a person who buys things.

Supermarkets

Can you imagine going shopping and having to queue up at a different counter for everything you want? This is what people had to do before supermarkets opened. A Tesco store was the first supermarket in Britain. It opened in 1956.

At first the customers hated it. They did not know what to do.

Can you read the notice just inside the door of this shop? Look carefully at the back of the store. Can you see another notice that says 'Also Counter Service'? This shop is trying to keep its old customers as well as introducing the new way of shopping.

Soon most big shops changed to 'self-service' and people got used to it but many small local shops found that the number of their customers went down.

Television

Many people, who could afford it, bought their first television set in 1953, the year of Queen Elizabeth's coronation. After that everyone wanted one.

Number of television sets in Britain

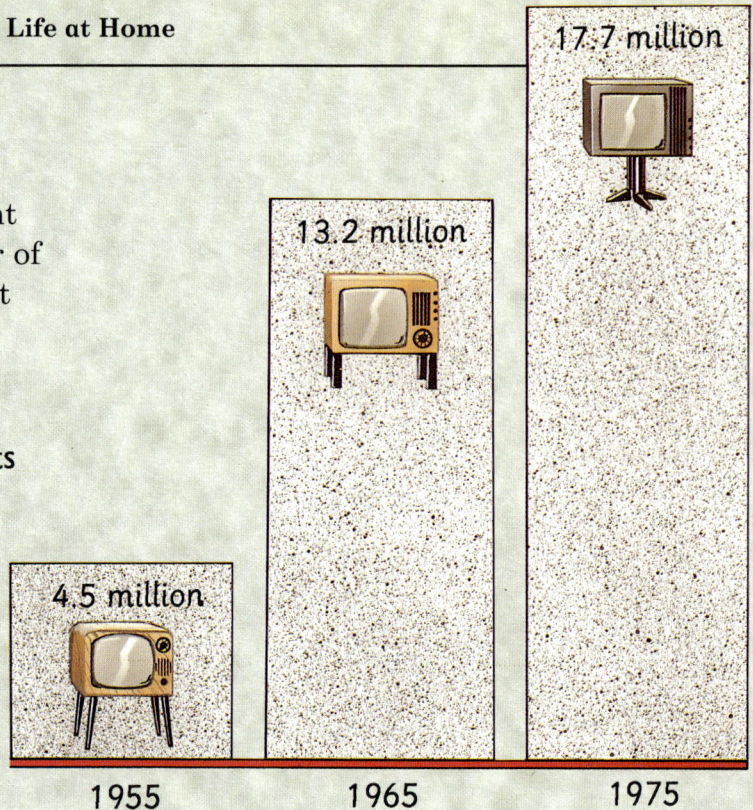

Look at this diagram. It shows how more and more homes got a television set. Find the differences:

◆ between 1955 and 1965.

◆ between 1965 and 1975.

◆ between 1955 and 1975.

17·7 million

13.2 million

4.5 million

1955   1965   1975

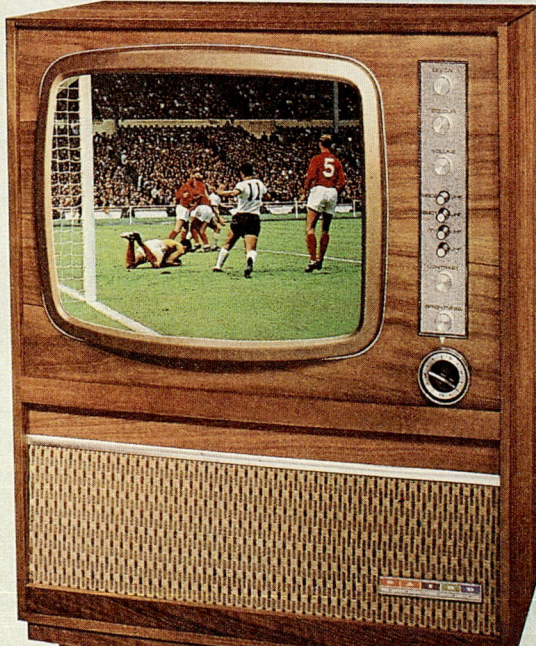

Most people rented their first television set. If it broke down the shop would mend it for nothing.

All the programmes were put out by the BBC until 1955 when a new channel called ITV began. It showed the first adverts.

Colour television started in Britain in 1967.

The rent for this set is in old money which changed in 1971.

◆ **Does your TV set look like the one in the picture?**

◆ **Do you think people thought this was a good offer?**

Pop Music

In the 1960s people could
listen to pop music on the
radio or television and then
go out and buy the record.
This was the first time they
had been able to do this.

**This group made their
first record in 1962. The
song was called 'Love
me do', which is still
often played today.**

♦ **Who were they? Have
you heard them sing?**

TOP FIFTY

1. **THE NEXT TIME/BACHELOR BOY**
   Cliff Richard. Columbia
2. **RETURN TO SENDER** .... Elvis Presley. RCA
3. **DANCE ON!** .... Shadows. Columbia
4. **SUN ARISE** .... Rolf Harris. Columbia
5. **GUITAR MAN** .... Duane Eddy. RCA
6. **LOVESICK BLUES/SHE TAUGHT ME HOW TO
   YODEL** .... Frank Ifield. Columbia
7. **TELSTAR** .... Tornados. Decca
8. **BOBBY'S GIRL** .... Susan Maughan. Philips
9. **LET'S DANCE** .... Chris Montez. London
10. **IT ONLY TOOK A MINUTE** .... Joe Brown. Piccadilly
11. **SWISS MAID** .... Del Shannon. London
12. **ROCKIN' AROUND THE CHRISTMAS TREE**
    Brenda Lee. Brunswick
13. **A FOREVER KIND OF LOVE** .... Bobby Vee. Liberty
14. **DESAFINADO** .... Stan Getz and Charlie Byrd HMV
15. **THE MAIN ATTRACTION** .... Pat Boone. London
16. **LIKE I DO** .... Maureen Evans. Oriole
17. **DEVIL WOMAN** .... Marty Robbins. CBS
18. **UP ON THE ROOF** .... Kenny Lynch. HMV
19. **GO AWAY LITTLE GIRL** .... Mark Wynter. Pye
20. **YOUR CHEATING HEART** .... Ray Charles. HMV
21. **LOVE ME DO** .... Beatles. Parlophone
22. **SHERRY** .... Four Seasons. Stateside
23. **MUST BE MADISON** .... Joe Loss. HMV
24. **BABY TAKE A BOW** .... Adam Faith. Parlophone
25. **CAN CAN '62** .... Peter Jay. Decca
26. **VENUS IN BLUE JEANS** .... Mark Wynter. Pye
27. **HE'S A REBEL** .... Crystals. London
28. **ME AND MY SHADOW**
    Frank Sinatra and Sammy Davis. Reprise
29. **LOVE ME TENDER** ...... Richard Chamberlain. MGM
30. **ISLAND OF DREAMS** .... Springfields. Philips
31. **BECAUSE OF LOVE** .... Billy Fury. Decca
32. **JAMES BOND THEME** .... John Barry. Columbia
33. **WE'RE GONNA GO FISHIN'** ...... Hank Locklin. RCA
34. **GOSSIP CALYPSO** .... Bernard Cribbins. Parlophone
35. **JUST FOR KICKS** ...... Mike Sarne. Parlophone
36. **NO ONE CAN MAKE MY SUNSHINE SMILE**
    Everly Brothers. Warner Bros.
37. **I REMEMBER YOU** .... Frank Ifield. Columbia
38. **UP ON THE ROOF** .... Julie Grant. Pye
39. **THE LOCO-MOTION** .... Little Eva. London
40. **LIMBO ROCK** ...... Chubby Checker. Cameo-Parkway

Many new groups started in the 1960s and
people spent much more of their time
listening to their favourite groups and going
to concerts. British groups were popular all
over the world and performed in front of
huge crowds.

Ask your mum or dad if they have any old
records by these stars.

**Here are some names
of groups who were
in the 'chart' in the
1960s as well as the
Beatles.**

29

Fashion

There have been many changes in fashion since the Second World War. Here are just a few of them. To find out more look through your family's old photographs and ask them about the clothes they had.

This was the first new fashion after the war. It started in Paris and was called the New Look.

This is the style of dress most women wore. Like the New Look it had a narrow waist and a full skirt. Underneath a net petticoat was worn to make the skirt stand out. Women did not wear trousers in 1957 when this dress was made.

Most men and women remember the miniskirt in the 1960s. Mary Quant was one of the designers who made it fashionable.

♦ What differences can you see in this dress and the New Look style?

This was the new fashion as long ago as 1953. The first jeans came from America so not many people could buy them until they began to be made in Britain.

Look at the woman in the picture. No one then thought women would ever buy jeans.

In the 1960s young men and women had more money to spend. Their favourite clothes were like those worn by the pop stars. Men's clothes got more casual and colourful and they also started to wear their hair long.

Some young men and women wore clothes like these. They called themselves 'hippies' and said they belonged to the 'flower power' movement which campaigned for 'Peace'. One of the people they admired was the Beatle, John Lennon.

Look carefully at the photo.

♦ **What else do you think fashionable young men and women liked wearing when they went out?**

Other Changes in Post-war Britain

In this book you have read about some of the ways things have changed in post-war Britain but there are many more things to investigate.

Here are some things to do:

— Ask your mum, dad or grandparents what happened to them in the 1950s, 1960s, 1970s or 1980s.

— Go to your local library and ask to see some old newspapers.

— Find out what was happening in your area at the time.

— Look at the advertisements too.

— Look for post-war estates and post-war schools. Talk to people who remember when they were first built. Then try to work out what has changed and what has stayed the same.

— Think about changes that are happening now and what people at school in a hundred years time will find out about us!